6/13 2-41. UTD 5/13

House Beautiful
The Apartment Book

House Beautiful

The Apartment Book

Smart Decorating for Spaces Large and Small

CAROL SPIER

Hearst Books

A Division of Sterling Publishing Co., Inc.

New York

Library of Congress Cataloging-in-Publication Data

Spier, Carol.
   The apartment book : smart decorating for spaces large and small / Carol Spier.
          p. cm.
Includes bibliographical references and index.
ISBN-13: 978-1-58816-598-5 (alk. paper)
ISBN-10: 1-58816-598-1 (alk. paper)
 1.   Apartments. 2.   Interior decoration.   I. Title.
NK2195.A6S65 2007
747'.88314—dc22

2006029559

10 9 8 7 6 5 4 3 2 1

Book design by Celia Fuller

Published by Hearst Books
A Division of Sterling Publishing Co., Inc.
387 Park Avenue South, New York, NY 10016

House Beautiful and Hearst Books are trademarks of Hearst Communications, Inc.

www.housebeautiful.com

For information about custom editions, special sales, premium and corporate purchases, please contact Sterling Special Sales Department at 800-805-5489 or specialsales@sterlingpub.com.

Distributed in Canada by Sterling Publishing
c/o Canadian Manda Group, 165 Dufferin Street
Toronto, Ontario, Canada M6K 3H6

Distributed in Australia by Capricorn Link (Australia) Pty. Ltd.
P.O. Box 704, Windsor, NSW 2756 Australia

Manufactured in China

Sterling ISBN 13: 978-1-58816-598-5
          ISBN 10: 1-58816-598-1

CONTENTS

INTRODUCTION

The classic quandary of how to make a house a home is as applicable to an apartment as it is to a freestanding residence. You probably know this if you are reading this book—you are or soon will be an apartment dweller—and you look forward to living in a space that is comfortable, convenient, and attractive, a space filled with the style and ambiance you find appealing and reflective of you.

Small apartments may have less space than a small house, but large ones rival grand houses in scale. So size is not really the difference between an apartment and a house; the limitations, advantages, and challenges of space are the same in both. Ownership is not a difference either; you may own your co-op or condo while others may rent a house. Apartment dwellers do have some unique issues and concerns: proximity to neighbors that brings issues of privacy and noise; a limited number of exterior walls to offer windows for light and ventilation; a lack of control over building operations; shared mechanical systems; and public hallways, elevators, and doormen. Residents of large buildings may be high above the street with great views and perhaps a balcony—hardly negatives! Loft dwellers enjoy large spaces, often only minimally divided—a plus for your sense of freedom, a minus when you're trying to create a bedroom and can't figure out how to bring natural light into the enclosure. And if you inhabit a studio apartment, chances are you are not only pressed for space, you're looking at everything you own no matter where you sit.

Basic Questions Give You a Smart Start

Begin your decorating plan by answering some basic questions: *Do you rent or own, and how long do you expect to live in the apartment?* The answer may affect the feasibility of major changes or the size of the investment you make. *How old is your building, and what mechanical challenges will you face?* There may be structural,

electrical, or plumbing restrictions or obstacles. *How accessible is your apartment?* Walk-ups are more awkward to update than first-floor or elevator apartments; building management, doormen, and superintendents may be friends or foes to workmen. *What kind of change do you want to make?* If it's just cosmetic, your task may be easy. If it's a gut and redo, how will you cope while the work is in process? *Will you plan the change yourself, or hire a designer?* However you answer this last query, the clearer your ideas for what you want to do, the smoother the process will be and the better its results.

Dream, Design, Decorate

The Apartment Book is filled with ideas for turning your apartment into your home. Six chapters devoted to individual rooms—Living Rooms, Dining Areas, Kitchens, Bathrooms, Bedrooms, and Libraries, Offices, and Entryways—feature numerous photographs of apartment interiors in every scale, decorated in many styles. You'll see terrific tiny kitchens, spacious lofts, modest living rooms, and grand dining rooms. At the end of each chapter are special features with ideas for solving common problems, like storage or the challenges of living in a small space, plus information and inspiration for displaying collections or using color. Tips are sprinkled among the photographs. Browse, read, and note the photos that appeal to you. And be open—it's easy to pass over a good idea because you don't care for the style, color, or material used to execute it. Consider whether that shelf tucked below a kitchen window might be just the thing to solve your display problem before you dismiss it because you don't like stainless steel. Take a look; you're sure to find a space that looks like home.

LIVING ROOMS

1

Welcoming, relaxing, comfortable, gathering place. Your living room no doubt shares with the dining room the responsibility of being the most public part of your apartment—elegant or informal, expansive or intimate, it's a place where you entertain. When decorating it, your first goal is probably to provide comfortable seating arranged to invite conversation; with planning and an educated eye you can take that a step further and put together furnishings that share your hospitable spirit and reflect your taste in design and art.

Apartment living rooms come in all shapes and sizes, and while the challenges of decorating a small one differ from a grander room, there are two steps that get any living room off to a good start: Choose a style that will give the ambiance you wish, and determine how to focus the layout. Your choice of style is mostly personal, but it could be guided by the architectural period of your apartment or by your locale. In addition, your style preference will depend on whether your apartment includes the luxury of a family room or den as well as a living room, and whether children will frequent the room. Your choice of layout, on the other hand, is dependent on the configuration of the space—square or rectangular, large or small, and its relationship to other areas of the apartment—and on features such as a fireplace or view that you'd like to take advantage of or an object such as a piano or large painting that is to be incorporated. There is probably more than one good way to arrange things;

OPPOSITE: A low back makes this small, chunky sofa a good choice for a small apartment—it's comfy and crosses the opening between dining and living rooms without closing up the visual space. One tone-on-tone papered interior wall is fun; with the other walls painted yellow or off-white, its allover pattern won't overwhelm.

just think about the way the traffic will flow, whether conversation will be easy and facilitated by one or more groupings of furniture, and how natural and artificial lighting will come into play.

As you plan your decorating, review the questions in the Introduction; they'll help you understand the scope of your project and determine whether the work is a wise investment of time and resources for you as a renter or owner. Furniture can be moved with you or sold; paint, wallpaper, and built-ins cannot, and structural modification to your space adds another dimension to your project. Consider your responsibility as a neighbor too: Are you taking proper steps to muffle your sound system? Will your window treatments shield neighbors from unwitting participation in your life?

As you look through the photos in this chapter you'll see many inviting options for living room design in both traditional and individual styles. Flag the ones that appeal to you. Make a list of your goals: a whole new look, a facelift, better reading light, a mural, or a place to display your collection of ceramics. Read the special features, "Getting the Hang of Artwork," "Color Concepts," and "Twelve Tricks That Make Your Space Look Larger." Make a plan for creating your ideal living room, follow through with it, and live happily in your new space.

TIP: Use pattern sparingly in a small room—too much will vibrate like a television test screen.

OPPOSITE: Furnishings with a low profile and simple lines set against a clean background of creamy white and light yellow make this very small room seem larger than it is. There are just a few sculptural accessories here and in the adjacent dining room; they share or accent the palette, add vertical lines, and fit well despite their relatively large scale.

OPPOSITE: With the seating area centered on the fireplace and a window bay on the adjacent wall, one corner of this room offers an ideal spot for a bookshelf or a display area. In this case, the fashion-designer owner chose to display two important tools of her home-based trade.

ABOVE: Dark stain on the parquet floor complements the faux granite finish on this Victorian carved mantel and throws it into stark relief against the white walls; the contrast is graphic and the mood contemporary. The upper ledge is set at the same height as the mantel, creating the illusion of an extended mantel. Black-and-white photos in narrow black frames complete the gallery effect.

ABOVE: Stripped of paint, the carved stone mantel shares the neutral palette of the other furnishings. The large mirror tosses light from the bank of windows across the space. Decorative paneling adds texture to the neutral color scheme.

LEFT: Old and new mix comfortably in this updated classic city apartment. New half-walls and a mezzanine open onto the living room where the original windows and fireplace mantel frame contemporary furnishings. Note the wide roller shade mounted at the ceiling.

ABOVE: Above the dado, the walls are painted in a grid of perpendicular striée squares, and framed graphics hang at eye level, suspended from the crown molding. The soft, restful colors in this room are an elegant choice for the blend of old with new.

OPPOSITE: An area carpet and luxuriously cushioned contemporary seating center a conversation area by the fireside in this living room, which is tall, narrow, and features grand moldings as is typical in a period row house. A recamier in the bay window works for solitary relaxation or joins the group.

TIP: To let your windows admit maximum light into a room, keep curtains as spare as possible.

ABOVE: Furniture resembling huge, bright pieces of candy sits in friendly anticipation of company in the grandly proportioned living room of this large loft. The unusual home office tucked in the corner is complementary and seems right at home.

OPPOSITE: Paired curtain panels are a smart choice for casement windows that open from the center. These hang to the floor from rods high inside the window; as sheer curtains, they filter the light and view but don't provide nighttime privacy.

RIGHT: Lots of white and a mix of solid-color and simple graphic fabrics keep this traditionally furnished living room fresh and up-to-date. The grid arrangement of frameless paintings is arresting without being busy or overwhelming.

TIP: Banish fussy window treatments from small rooms; hang simple panels or a crisp Roman shade with a contrasting border.

RIGHT: Blue and white is a classic decorating scheme. Here, white Roman shades edged in blue make jaunty toppers to the pair of windows at the end of the room. The wide, cushioned banquette below them conceals radiators and adds seating for good conversation or observation of the street scene outside.

ABOVE: A modular unit opposite the sofa continues the square theme; it's fitted with rattan baskets for pullout storage that is easy and good looking.

ABOVE: A tall folding screen covered in a tile-patterned fabric reiterates the colors, injects pattern into the square theme, and enhances the modernist furnishings.

OPPOSITE: This décor pays homage to the square in a palette of orange, brown, and ecru—even the square coffee table is topped with copper. The diagonal orientation of ceiling and rug patterns makes the room seem larger. Furnishings in solid-color fabrics, including the traditional curtains, keep the focus on the walls, floor, and ceiling.

ABOVE: A love of color and Asian and Middle Eastern accoutrements provides the raison d'être for this exuberant décor, which proves that more is more as long as there is lots of variety balanced by a few repeated themes.

ABOVE: Painted all white, this elaborate mantel is a great stage for showing off smaller treasures; the blue-violet wall displays the accessories of cobalt and white on the top shelf to best advantage.

ABOVE: The enormous marble slab surrounding the fireplace is as important as a piece of artwork and provides the only pattern in the décor; the rug and upholstery are softly textured.

RIGHT: Low-slung furniture keeps the view across the room to the windows open. Cabinets hide the heaters and provide storage. The pink chair is a fresh and lively burst of color.

TIP: Solid color upholstery highlights the form of your furniture—prints call more attention to themselves than to the chair or sofa they cover.

LEFT: A mixture of textures—matte, shiny, smooth, and nubby—and contrasting dark and pale colors add depth and interest to the clean lines of the furniture used in this sitting area. The huge mirror tosses light across the space. The leather chair is a Hans Wegner Papa Bear wing chair from the 1950s.

TIP: Show some leg— unskirted furniture gives an illusion of depth. Skirted furniture closes off a space.

ABOVE: Open, floating shelves and a curtain of large plastic discs frame the sides of the sitting area in this large loft, giving it a sense of enclosure. The monochrome décor is marked by symmetry and a near-total absence of accessories or artwork; light and air take center stage.

OPPOSITE: The leggy furniture and minimalist construction of the shelves barely interrupt the space. Another disc curtain hangs against the far wall; the circle motif is repeated in the coffee table, the floor beneath a dining counter, and again in the white wall clock.

LEFT: Soaring proportions and linear simplicity are the hallmarks of this living room, which fills one corner of a duplex apartment. Long, matching sofas face one another on opposite sides of the slate fireplace, which sits in handsome relief against the one expanse of wall. The honey-colored Eucalyptus trunk table adds a sculptural touch.

ABOVE: The living area is open to the kitchen and dining areas. The overall use of dark wood with white furnishings, punctuated only by a few honey-toned pieces (and no artwork), allows the drama of the space itself to dominate.

OPPOSITE: Both of these two-story exterior walls are permeated with light, which is intensified by the nearly all-white décor. The windows behind the sofa are fitted with discreet roller shades to mitigate the glare.

OPPOSITE: This colorful and comfortable media room occupies one-half of an open living room. Both areas are designed, while quite simply, to express a very personal sense of comfort and style.

BELOW: Like the chairs in the adjacent media room, the living room sofa is oversize, streamlined, and sculptural. Its low-back, L-shape design, is particularly suited to its position in front of the glass wall. Rugs, each different, define the two sitting areas; the transparent coffee table is cool and keeps the space open.

TIP: Lucite or glass is less obtrusive than wood for tables—a good trick for opening up a small room.

ABOVE: The den adjacent to the formal living room seen opposite features a wall of open and enclosed shelves which house books, the stereo, and a large television. Warm tones and comfortable furniture invite one to settle in and relax.

OPPOSITE: The owners of this large apartment dedicated adjacent areas to formal and informal living, separating the two with sliding wood panels. When the panels are open, as here, both rooms seem larger; when closed each is more intimate.

TIP: Think big in a small space—use overscale furniture to make it look larger.

OPPOSITE: The living room of this tiny Parisian apartment is lavishly furnished with elaborate period pieces. The limited palette—with lots of creamy white, gold, and a judicious use of green and rose—and the delicate proportions of the furniture and accessories are deftly combined to fill and flatter the very small room.

ABOVE: Large, elegantly framed mirrors (one here behind the settee and another over the mantel, seen opposite) enlarge the space, reflecting the furnishings and giving the illusion of distant walls.

ABOVE: A window wall blesses this L-shape studio with lots of light. The living and sleeping areas share the long side of the L-shape; the dining area is in the alcove with the kitchen (not seen here). The sofa is turned away from the dining table to create some separation and faces a media cabinet placed against one wall. In the foreground, a daybed with high head- and footboards creates a sense of privacy for the sleeping area.

LEFT: There's no pretense of large quarters here—it's one-room living, arranged with charm and focused on the marble mantel. The small sofa doubles as footboard to the bed in the bow window, the chairs are intriguing, and a very contemporary, freestanding closet has been tucked into the recesses next to the fireplace.

ABOVE: Modern furnishings work just as well as traditional ones in this elegant room; a change of light fixtures is important to the successful blend of old and new styles. The room feels larger, though no less defined, with two armchairs backing onto the adjacent space.

OPPOSITE: A long room containing both the living and dining areas seems even longer thanks to the mirror at the far end. A neutral palette keeps the room relaxed, while the glass lamp bases add touches of shimmer around the space. The dark color of the dining chairs and the frame around the mirror adds a bit of contrast to the neutral sofas.

ABOVE: An area carpet stops short of two structural columns to define and contain the sitting space; from the sofa, the columns frame the dining area beyond an interior passage.

BELOW: This sitting area couldn't be simpler. It is situated in the interior of a loft and open on all sides except behind the sofa. The contemporary furniture is eye-catching, and neutral tones keep it in harmony with the surroundings.

OPPOSITE: This room is tailored, soft, serene, and sophisticated with dove gray upholstery on the walls and matching sofas and differing gray tones on the floor, armchair, and ottoman, all offset by white accents.

RIGHT: Glowing gold and verdigris tones create a rich backdrop to this small seating area with a high ceiling. Gray, black, and honey-colored furnishings fit calmly into this space. The piecing of the full-length curtains introduces a horizontal element, a nice balance for the overall proportions.

TIP: Monochromatic color schemes are a great decorating device. To be most effective, they need at least three shades of the same color.

TIP: A flat-panel TV brings unobtrusive media into a sleek living space.

LEFT: Clean lines, rich but low-key colors, and just a few striking accessories complement this raised hearth of polished stone slabs. Together with a fireplace surround of stacked, natural stone, they take center stage in this contemporary living room.

LEFT: A diagonal arrangement allows a fair number of boxy pieces to sit lightly in this small, square room. The lamp introduces additional diagonals while the tubular metal armchairs keep the space feeling open. The easel is an ideal way to show off a piece of art.

ABOVE: A period game table tucked next to the fireplace adds old-world contrast; another mirror tops the framed print. Well designed, practical furnishings add a touch of luxury to any room.

OPPOSITE: A witty blend of traditional and exotic tastes sets the tone in this small apartment where elegant furnishings sit amid the blue-and-white zebra-pattern wallpaper. Vivid wallpaper picks up light and can make a small room look larger. The furniture is small in scale as befits the space, and the textiles kept quite plain to relieve the busy background.

ABOVE: The firebox is plain and painted black, the mantel is a slab of marble on brackets attached through the mirror, the hearth is polished black marble.

OPPOSITE: The leopard pillow subtly echoes the junge theme. A mirrored wall around the fireplace opens up this end of the room. A large, gilt-framed mirror is hung on the mirrored wall—a nice touch that brings a period sensibility to a modern convention. Inexpensive but luxurious brown bamboo matting is soft underfoot and easy to keep clean.

ABOVE: Rooms decorated in blue and white always seem fresh and crisp. Here, the colors define the living area centered in a large, multipurpose room. Note the informal coffee table—it's a camp bed with a striped mattress.

LEFT: Fearless pink walls declare this a very personal space put together by someone with an unerring eye for color, which makes possible a successful mix of such eclectic furnishings in a grand and formal room.

ABOVE: Natural wood tones and white make an easy backdrop; if the furniture is also white, you'll find that even a bit of color really pops. The décor here is simple and comfortable; the bouquet and rose-colored pillows warm it up.

OPPOSITE: Deeply colored walls, often in red or green hues, are traditional choices when intimacy is the desired effect in a living room, den, or library. Here, a highly glazed, red-on-red ragged finish is cheery when reflecting sunlight and turns cozy when the curtains are pulled and lamplight glows.

ABOVE: With the chimneypiece painted white to match the walls, this mantel disappears while the objects on it come into focus. The dark hearth and firewall are balanced by the cordovan leather chair, while the red lamp base stands brightly on a dark side table.

TIP: Use sliding panels or curtains hung from the ceiling to create flexible spaces within a large loft.

ABOVE: A deep pile carpet softens the austere modernity of this décor. An unobtrusive ceiling track allows the curtain behind the sofa to divide the room or be pushed back to hang like an architectural column.

OPPOSITE: An enormous mirror, framed in black and leaned casually against the wall, highlights the tailored furnishings—largely ecru, with gold and black accents—to give this room its relaxed elegance. The pictures perched on the sofa back enhance the effect but may not be practical for everyday display.

OPPOSITE: A window recess, square area rug, and L-shape sofa define the sitting room in one corner of this large open space, and a pale palette reinforces the spaciousness. Note how the cabinet at one end of the sofa provides great display space and balances the slight asymmetry of the setup.

ABOVE: Dark colors and invitingly plump, oversize pieces are an unexpected solution to the challenge of a small living room. This design is very efficient—settle in to relax and even dine—and the large mirror, light walls, and full-length curtains soften the black sofa.

OPPOSITE: At first glance Bohemian chic seems to rule this room, but a second look reveals that the use of pattern, while important, is fairly restrained. The mirrored folding screen gives focus to the corner sitting area and makes all the details wonderful—three times over.

ABOVE: Daylight enters this inviting spot from the wall opposite the armoire, filling the room with sunshine. The armoire is a bar; hence the adjacent shelves stocked with glasses. The nineteenth-century mirror frames are a combination of wood and studded leather.

TIP: Wood—painted, gilded, or natural—adds gentle warmth to a room.

ABOVE: A matched pair of 1950s chairs—one at the window and a second angled slightly away from it—await reading or conversation. The table is a modern classic by George Nakashima. Curtains flank the window, which frames a quintessential urban view.

OPPOSITE: Low-key and low slung, the chair opposite this traditional English sofa is paired with a side table that is a small wooden cube; the sofa is matched with a coffee table in the shape of a drum. Small floor lamps complete the uncomplicated décor in white and earth tones.

ABOVE: This booklover's sitting room has terrific full-length windows, which make it seem larger than it is. The angled seating brings guests together for a tête-à-tête; solid-color upholstery gives each piece a modern poise despite the assorted period styles.

OPPOSITE: A big mirror leaning against the wall captures filtered sunlight and adds a charming background to one end of the room. The ottoman can double as a coffee table.

ABOVE: A large map of Paris, cut up and mounted in a grid of individually framed sections, fills the space above the plain shelves at the end of this small sitting area. Its dusky monotone and visual texture are fine complements to the handsome taupe, gray, and yellow room.

LEFT: The large painting dominates one wall of this loft living area. Apart from the mix of modern and Asian furnishing, the carpet offers the only other pattern, and the arrangement keeps eyes focused on the art and permits easy access to it.

ABOVE: Although centered on the window and within its space, this furniture arrangement has a pleasant asymmetry, designed to showcase the single piece of art that fills the wall behind the side chairs. The floor cushion provides extra seating while keeping the room open to the adjacent area.

OPPOSITE: The taupe and honey tones of the walls and furnishings complement the smoky, reflective surface of the art, providing a more integrated setting than stark white.

ABOVE: Oversized to the point of nearly dwarfing its surroundings, this artwork is perfectly balanced in its space and claims the attention it deserves—larger furniture would be out of scale and spoil the effect.

OPPOSITE: A substantial frame anchors the graphic centered over this sofa; a small, delicate molding would be out of scale in this setting. The row of snapshots below is fun and fits neatly in its space.

TIP: Oversize paintings open up a room, creating a vista or second window, especially if there is no view.

ABOVE: Symmetrical arrangements are satisfying, and the less rigid the pairing, the livelier they are. With fun colors, witty patterns, and a rather offbeat style mix, this setup delights the eye. The small shades on the floor lamps provide just the right fill for the spaces between the painting and the end tables.

OPPOSITE: Asymmetrical arrangements invite the eye to travel rather than focus on a central point. This one is well balanced and leads you on a diagonal journey from the blue square on the right side of the painting, to the bolster, and then up to the small figure on the tall post, or down to the lower blue pedestal.

RIGHT: In this light-filled room, a huge framed mirror propped against the wall tricks the eye in masquerade as a third window. The view it reflects, however, is the apartment interior and anyone approaching the sitting area.

OPPOSITE: Sparkling like a marvelous, giant brooch pinned above the sofa, this elaborate mirrored frame demands attention. Unlike a large framed mirror, it doesn't reflect and expand the space—its role is to dazzle.

RIGHT: This mirror is the same width as the settee beneath it and fills the classic role of a large mirror—it makes the small room seem larger and brighter, and being framed, is decorative in its own right.

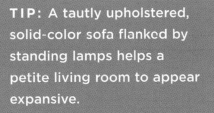

TIP: A tautly upholstered, solid-color sofa flanked by standing lamps helps a petite living room to appear expansive.

ABOVE: In this large room, a hallway of sorts exists between the sofa back and the painting hung opposite it. The wall at the end of this space has been fitted with discreet shelves (one at counter height) and a table behind the sofa gives a sense of purpose to the walkway.

OPPOSITE: Bookshelves rim the perimeter of this duplex loft where old and new mix stylishly, and various seating groups play host individually or as a group. Pilasters framing the shelf bays echo the columns that punctuate the space; both shelves and pilaster capitals are neatly fitted under the stairs.

OPPOSITE: The thoughtfully designed built-in unit serves as an unobtrusive media wall. The strategic combination of open cubes, sliding doors, and assorted drawers is both handy and good-looking.

ABOVE: This small space has been set up as a den; there is just enough room for a coffee table between the sofa on one wall and the modular shelves on the other. The bookshelf tower on the end wall balances the wood panel to the left of the window.

TIP: If you can't afford to install built-in cabinetry to create streamlined storage, try lining up several tall bookcases.

ABOVE: The translucent panels that separate this combination office and den from the adjacent living area keep light flowing and slide shut to provide privacy as needed. Built-in cupboards below the window abut the curved desk; the convex profile of the desk provides a larger surface, easier access to the view, and keeps anyone seated there from feeling stuck in the corner.

ABOVE: The media cabinet doors mimic the sliding panels and minimize the mass of the storage unit. The coffee table is an architect's flat file, which its owner had fitted with casters and a piece of glass cut to fit the top.

OPPOSITE: With a wall of shelves as a backdrop, this seating group gathered around a pedestal table invites discussion of a good book or hosts an intimate tea party. Note the sconces on the shelf casing: They illuminate the books, photographs, and loveseat.

ABOVE: A "great room" it may not be, but this combination living/library/dining area, which opens from a kitchen to the left, serves the same purpose. Family life centers here happily, if compactly, and the cook is never isolated. The broad horizontal stripes on the wall keep your eye moving around the small space.

Before and After:
Opened and Updated

Before

Dark floors and heavy curtains made this living
room seem dark, despite the two big windows at
the end of the room. Although a large space,
it felt closed in to the owner, who disliked its
isolation from the rest of the apartment. In fact,
the chief drawback of the apartment was its
layout—the only entry to any room was through an interior hall.

After

In a triumph of demolition that dispelled the room's cavernous feeling, nearly half
the wall between the living room and adjacent dining room was knocked down and
replaced with a sliding, translucent door. Now both spaces share the light from their
windows, and people and conversation move freely from one room to the next.

1 Steel radiator covers, now stripped and burnished, pay a nice compliment to the
sliding-door frame. They're topped by a long maple shelf, which spans the
width of the room.

2 The dividing door slides into a pocket in the wall, so it disappears when fully
open. When closed, light still passes through it.

3 The windows, once blocked by curtains, are now veiled with solar shades,
which let the sunlight in while minimizing glare and maintaining the view.

4 To bridge the change in level between the two rooms, a broad step was added
below the sliding door.

5 Simple lines and a palette of light, neutral tones make the furnishings appear to
float in the airy space.

GETTING THE HANG OF ARTWORK

1. **Balance.** Arranging photos and paintings is an art—the mix of proportions, textures, and colors should look balanced of itself and in relation to the wall space and nearby furnishings. Work with a friend so one of you can hold the piece while the other appraises the location and balance.

2. **Density.** Hang photos or paintings close together to make the effect of the whole greater than the sum of the individual pieces.

3. **Mock it up.** Work out the relative positions in a group display by laying the pieces out on the floor.

4. **Hook right.** Hold a picture by the center of its wire and measure from the wire to the top of the frame; install the hanger so the bottom of the hook is that distance from the desired top of the picture.

5. **Mix the media.** It's okay for paintings, watercolors, prints, drawings, and photos to coexist in a single arrangement.

6. **Serial framing.** If the graphics are part of a series, or you want them to have a mass impact, use matching frames for all.

7. **Frame to suit.** To avoid a mass-produced look and complement individual artworks, use a unique frame for each piece.

8. **Gallery hallway.** Line a hallway or foyer with artwork to create a gallery—guests will pause and look instead of rushing through.

9. **Alignment is optional.** Framed photos and paintings need not be perfectly aligned on a wall. Choose a configuration that works with the architecture and other furnishings.

10. **Meant to be seen.** Choose eye-level display for smaller pieces, especially if they're hung individually.

COLOR CONCEPTS

Color sets the tone and influences mood. Some decorating styles are associated with specific color palettes while others welcome the full spectrum. Color preference is personal—use color to express yourself.

Color changes with the light. When you choose specific paint hues and textiles or wallpaper, look at samples in your space under different lighting conditions. • Wood, stone, and metal, of course, have color, too. • Surface plays a role as well: Reflective surfaces like glass or glazed tile make colors sparkle, and absorbent surfaces like wood, honed stone, or velvet soften their effect.

Volume affects intensity. The more there is of a color, the more intense it will appear. • Use strong, bright colors with intention, as accents to enliven discretely or in swathes to make a passionate statement. • Carry a single color scheme throughout a small apartment to create a sense of openness and continuity that flows from one room to the next.

Painted color tricks: Moldings need not be painted a contrasting color. When architectural detail is elaborate (or moldings are in less-than-perfect condition), using one flat-finish color on everything will result in a more elegant look.   Paint radiators to match the walls to make them less obtrusive.   Use metallic paint to open up a long, dark hallway. Silvers and golds reflect light and make the space brighter.   A painted ceiling influences ambiance without interrupting the eye—pink for warmth, sky blue for openness, and midnight blue, silver, or gold for drama.   One intensely colored wall in an all-white or neutral room will recede and add dimension to the space.

Accessory color tricks: Add colored lampshades; they can be custom-made from fabric or paper in almost any color imaginable. • Use a colorful rug to enliven a drab or quiet room—it will ground the space and add depth and drama. Use a neutral rug to offset strong color elsewhere. • Stretch a colorful quilt over an artist's canvas frame and hang it on a wall to add an instant shot of color. • Frame a print with a mat that matches one of the artwork's dominant colors. • Go for colorful slipcovers—they're not permanent, so you can change them to suit the season or a new mood. • Pick one color to accent a monochrome décor, then use it for pillows, a vase, a bowl, even fresh flowers—let your collection of yellowware, Jade-ite, or blue-and-white ceramics indicate the choice. • Use one wonderfully multicolored textile or painting to set the palette for the room, repeating its hues individually on other furnishings.

TWELVE TRICKS THAT MAKE YOUR SPACE LOOK LARGER

1. **Decorate with intention.** Haphazard décor just accentuates the shoebox effect of a small space.

2. **Round tables work well.** They're easy to walk around and you can always squeeze in an extra chair. Plus, they look fine if they're off center on a wall or in front of a sofa.

3. **Lateral accents expand the space.** Paint your walls with horizontal bands in three related colors or several sheens of the same hue.

4. **Mirrors open up small spaces.** Many mirrors set at different angles open up a room even more and reflect bits and pieces of things you might not otherwise notice.

5. **Use many small sources of light.** Lampshades that concentrate the light give the impression that a space is larger.

6. **Leave the ceiling unlit or you'll feel it's on your head.** Several small lamps will add character and depth to the room.

7. **Use light furniture with legs.** Skirted furniture closes up a space.

8. **Create perspectives so you don't feel closed in**. The view from one room to another should be intentionally composed with a smooth transition from one ambiance to the next.

9. **Add interior windows** (open spaces in a wall) to allow light, air, and conversation to pass from room to room.

10. **Keep the eye moving.** Make window treatments and walls the same color.

11. **Get rid of doors wherever you can.** Replace them if you like with light curtains—funky ones made of light-bulb pull chains or strung beads could be just the thing.

12. **Go for things of good quality.** In a small space everything receives attention.

DINING AREAS

2

Inviting, festive, relaxing, elegant, and informal by turns. Whether you have a dining room, dining area, or a table in a nook that does double duty as desk, the place where you dine should be welcoming and comfortable. The layout of your apartment and the way you live and entertain influence the way you decorate your dining room: if it's used for breakfast, lunch, and dinner, you'll furnish it differently than one reserved for formal entertaining, and if your dining room is part of a large living space, you'll have different, and limited, options for its design. Unless you reserve your dining room for formal entertaining, chances are you want it to be flexible, so take advantage of the versatility inherent in dining décor and use a variety of linens and tableware to give it different looks, and change the ambiance with candlelight, a chandelier, sconces, or sunlight.

Stand in the doorway or at the edge of your dining space and think about its configuration, proportions, and architectural features. Is the ceiling high or low? Where are the windows? Is there a fireplace? Is the space intimate or grand? Think about how you use it: Does it house your library, and is artwork important to the décor? Do you host buffets or serve at the table? If it is not a separate room, how do you want to define it within the larger space? Is it an alcove? And are there columns, a raised or sunken area, or a counter on which to center it? Or is the space so open that simply placing the table and chairs will create a dining area, and if so, what else

OPPOSITE: Against white walls and a built-in cabinet that matches the floor, and with accessories kept to a minimum, the full sculptural impact of this 1950s mahogany table and matching chairs is immediately apparent. A blue door sculpture is a whimsical part of this apartment dweller's art collection.

happens in the space, and what is the best way to accommodate its other functions and optimize the flow from one zone to another? Or is the space so small that you're not quite sure you even have a dining area?

However the nature and size of your dining area affect the way you set it up, your enjoyment of it will center on the table and chairs that welcome you to good food and conversation, and their proportion to the room is critical—too large and the effect will be crowded or clumsy; too small and the dining area will look lonely. Consider not only the visual proportions, but if your space is small, make sure there is room to pull chairs away from the table or pass behind seated diners to serve or clear the table.

To begin your decorating plan, answer the basic questions posed in the Introduction. You'll gain some insight about the scope of your project and, especially if you are considering structural changes, be able to judge whether your plan makes sense for you as a renter or owner. Then gather your design ideas—you'll find lots of inspiration for all kinds of dining areas in the photos in this chapter. Be sure to read the special features, "Ten Ways to Show Off a Collection" and "Well Lit." Make your choices and drink a toast to your new dining room.

OPPOSITE: An orange table runner adds a splash of color and texture to this dining area. The white chairs are stylish touch, and together with the dark table make a pretty and modern composition, perfect for entertaining guests.

OPPOSITE: This room was originally a bedroom. A square table oriented diagonally in a corner makes the small room seem spacious and allows traffic to flow. The pattern on the uphostery mimics the lattice-back chairs. Mid-tone wood, low, open chair backs, and light-colored accessories against the window contribute to the airy effect.

ABOVE: Count an alcove with French doors as an architectural blessing that will grace many a meal. Sunny colors and ornamental metal grilles create a Mediterranean ambiance, but whatever style of furnishings you choose, you can't go wrong with a setting like this.

TIP: Add drama by staining or painting your floor a rich hue—Chinese red, periwinkle, bottle green, or even black.

ABOVE: A long, narrow dining space— especially one with a doorway in each corner—doesn't give you much room to play, so accept the limits and center your furnishings on an end wall. This white-on-white room is light and airy, and it celebrates the rectilinear with the table, cabinet, and graphics. The chairs are a bright accent that enliven the space.

ABOVE: Tones of a single light color on walls, floor, and furnishings make a small space look commodious. In this dining area, which is partially defined by a pilaster on the rear wall, the area rug makes an asset of an awkward spatial transition. The round pedestal table appears delicate yet will accommodate additional chairs.

TIP: If your moldings are uninteresting, paint them the same color as the walls— they'll disappear and your room will look bigger, too.

OPPOSITE: If your space has assorted wall surfaces like the brick and wallboard in this loft, acknowledge them when you hang artwork. The white wall offers a clean background; its nicely designed niche adds a subtle frame to a display of objects as well as a portrait. The brick is busy; the abstract painting is both a strong accent and the perfect complement to its texture.

ABOVE, RIGHT: Here, an all-white paint treatment minimizes the moldings, making the walls a less important backdrop for the streamlined lamps that frame the clean lines of the sideboard and dining table. The composition is punctuated with graphic red lampshades that lead the eye to the painting.

TIP: A niche built into a wall functions like a window if it holds a painting, sculpture, or large textile— you'll perceive the display as a view.

ABOVE: If you want to minimize the distinction between the spaces in a loft, choose a table, chairs, sofa, coffee table, and easy chairs that share a design aesthetic—but don't be afraid of pieces with character. This unusual table adds visual texture and complements the overall use of clean lines and rich neutral hues against pale walls and curtains.

OPPOSITE: Enliven a neutral or monochromatic color scheme with an assortment of textures—the effect is quieter than a mix of patterns yet still interesting. Here, the wire open-weave chairs complement the rough brick wall and the metal radiator. The polished table is balanced by the sheen of the mirror, and the carpet and blinds each add a bit of dimension.

ABOVE: The dining area in a small, open-plan apartment is often just any spot a table will fit. This one successfully sits between the kitchen and living areas with a single color scheme of pale wood, white, glass, and dusty green used throughout, unifying the three zones. The round table can be moved further into the room to accommodate guests.

OPPOSITE: A floor level change of one, two, or more steps provides an instant division of space in an apartment layout, creating a mezzanine effect that separates and defines the dining area without closing it off from the living room.

LEFT: An enormous mirror tricks the eye into perceiving this dining area at twice its actual size. Dining chairs in three styles around the mahogany and stainless-steel table introduce variety to the simple décor; a shared palette keeps the effect harmonious. Note the fabrics on the chairs—the slipcover is made of wool and the skirt is linen gauze.

TIP: To give the illusion of height, hang curtains from poles mounted as close to the ceiling as possible.

OPPOSITE: There's no better invitation to intimate dining than a table for two in front of a fireplace—especially in a small space that's decorated in a personal manner. Here, the walls have been draped with flat panels of white canvas, which accentuate an eclectic collection of furnishings.

ABOVE: In a small space a round table will usually feel less cumbersome than a square one in a small space. The ornate pedestal makes this handsome example a stylish choice for the dual role of library and dining table, and despite its mass, it sits comfortably in its corner.

ABOVE: A tiny dining area, thoughtfully designed, can be as inviting as a grand one. The corner banquette with soft cushions, a handsome table and chairs, the single large print centered behind the table, and charming display nooks high above all make this a delightful place to dine.

OPPOSITE: This graceful modern table and playful chairs are visually light yet strong enough to look balanced in this space with a high ceiling. The long, low-arch table is an amusing counterpoint to the more classically proportioned archway that leads from the neighboring room.

TIP: Use matching frames for artwork that is part of a series. Change the frame scale if the artwork varies in size, but maintain the style.

OPPOSITE: The built-in charm of a breakfast nook easily compensates for any awkwardness encountered when sliding between the table and fixed benches. A small arch entry provides this one with a natural frame for a display of pretty plates and platters on the wall above the table.

ABOVE: An upholstered, high-backed banquette provides comfortable seating that saves space in a tight spot. This one matches the wall to keep its corner looking as large as possible; a tiny pedestal table and generously matted artwork complete the uncluttered design.

Before and After:
Properly Proportioned

Before

This dining room has strong architectural details with its elegant moldings and high ceiling, but its original décor felt haphazard and a bit stodgy to the young couple who own it. The room was too cluttered with furniture, the easy chair was out of place, and the artwork almost out of sight atop the high ledge. But good news, the challenge here was cosmetic, no structural changes were on order.

After

A neutral palette and furnishings with stature move the room into the modern world. Gone are the fussy carpet, delicate period dining set, casual slipcovered chair, and vivid blue ceiling. The new look is serene, uncluttered, and refined, yet not overly formal.

1. The ceiling recesses are now a pale, restful taupe.
2. Above the ledge, vertical stripe wallpaper (interesting, and unlike the pictures previously there, easily understood from below) lifts the eye to the ceiling.
3. Upholstered chairs and a table with heft hold their own against the moldings.
4. Artwork is centered on the panels and hung at eye level for greater impact and appreciation.
5. A textured, solid-color carpet echoes the creamy tones of the walls and ceiling and sets off the darker tones of the table and chairs.
6. The pendant light fixture and sconces are graphic, simple, and appropriately proportioned for the large room.

TEN WAYS TO SHOW OFF A COLLECTION

1. **Group it.** Separate items into small groupings of roughly equal mass, then arrange the groupings on a set of shelves.

2. **Stack them.** If you collect items with flat tops, place them one atop another, making several short towers; then arrange the towers on a shelf or bench.

3. **Consider proportion.** If one piece in your collection is much larger than the others, let it be the center of your display.

4. **Choose the right background.** Pick a color for the wall, cupboard, or case that complements and contrasts the color of your collection, or create an intentionally monochrome display.

5. **Contain small items.** Little treasures will be lost and swallowed in large areas. Arrange them on a tray, in a bowl, a curio cabinet, or another defined space.

6. **Find a rhythm.** Analyze the details of shape, pattern, or color in your collection; arrange items so these details alternate, mirror, or sit in rows in a pleasing way.

7. **Be a copycat.** Look in magazines, boutiques, and museums for display ideas; adapt them to your décor.

8. **Show them out of context.** Themed collections take on fresh meaning and gain sculptural impact if they're displayed in a room other than the one where they would be used.

9. **Layer with care.** When placing numerous items on a deep shelf, put larger pieces toward the back and overlap with smaller ones in front—make sure each can be appreciated.

10. **Light it.** Make sure there is appropriate illumination for your treasures to be appreciated in both the day and night, but be sure to protect them from direct sunlight.

WELL LIT

Every room needs three kinds of lighting: *natural* (from a window), *ambient* (from overhead fixtures and wall sconces), and *task* (from fixtures focused on a work or reading area; lighting for artwork or a hall table also falls into this category). Dimmer controls allow you to adjust ambient light. Flexible-arm fixtures are an enhancement for task lighting.

In an open-plan layout, a good lighting design will help create "rooms" where there are no walls.

Light can be warm or cool and affects the color and mood of the things it touches. The temperature of natural light varies with exposure (east, west, north, or south), time of day, and neighboring surroundings such as overhanging eaves, trees, or nearby buildings. The temperature of artificial light can be controlled by the kind of light bulb you use, and is also affected by the color of the lamp shade.

Lighting design is complex. Seek professional help if you don't know what to do (and most of us don't), especially if you are renovating a space. And if a fixture doesn't simply plug in, hire an electrician to install it legally and safely.

Figure lighting fixtures into your budget. While you may find the perfect (and perfectly priced) pendant, floor, or table lamp at the thrift shop or a trendy home store, the fixtures you really want may require an investment. Plan ahead for them—it's a shame to spoil a good decorating scheme with lamps purchased as an afterthought.

Lampshades are not one-size-fits-all. Take your lamp with you when purchasing a shade. And don't be shy if you don't see what you want; many vendors can arrange to have shades custom-made.

Style is a matter of taste. Modern light fixtures are wonderfully adaptive and look good with many styles of architecture and furnishings. You needn't be hung up on tradition—choose fixtures for the way their scale and materials fit with your other furnishings, as well as for their design lines.

KITCHENS

3

Efficient, up-to-date, inviting, roomy, the heart of the home. Fortunate are those who have such a kitchen, and who among us doesn't want one that fits this description? Apartment dwellers are often faced with kitchens that are small, bland, old, or isolated, but imagination and good planning can make this sort of unsatisfactory room welcoming and a pleasure to use, no matter its size or the size of your budget. In fact, a kitchen that looks perfect at first glance may be more of a challenge to make your own than one that's obviously problematic—you may not recognize the things that make it wrong for you or be reluctant to invest time or money altering something so apparently fine.

A well-designed kitchen—regardless of dimension, style, or budget—has the best possible arrangement of work space and appliances, organized, efficient storage, good lighting, and a welcoming ambiance. Of course, when it comes to space, more is almost always truly more in a kitchen, but if you accept reality, define your needs, and do some creative problem-solving, you can achieve very good—even perfect—results whatever the scale of your update.

Begin by answering the questions given in the Introduction—a reality check about the wisdom of investing in the apartment and the feasibility of making physical changes, not only to walls but also to plumbing and wiring, is especially important for kitchen updates, which can be both costly and disruptive. Your answers will give you some perspective on the scope of the project ahead of you, whether it's a simple

OPPOSITE: In this superbly organized kitchen, cooks are fortunate to have lots of work, storage, and walking space. Smaller rooms that are similarly filled will seem expansive if they borrow the pale colors, good lighting, and reflective surfaces of this design.

reorganization of the cabinets, a cosmetic makeover, a moderate renovation, or a complete gut and rebuild.

Next, move to the fun part and put together a plan. Gather your thoughts and ideas. List the challenges you face, the problems you want to solve, and the things you dislike about the kitchen as it is. Collect visual references for the way you want the kitchen to look. Don't confuse style with ideas: A counter or shelf cleverly fitted in an odd space, a great configuration of appliances, or a marvelously organized cupboard may be perfect for you once you look beyond materials or colors that are not to your taste. Go shopping to see options for whatever you plan to add. Ask questions of vendors and also of friends who have gear you like. Two things especially important—and easily overlooked—in an apartment kitchen are the exhaust system for the stove, because exterior walls may not be accessible, and the operating noise of appliances, which may permeate not only your space but your neighbors' as well.

The pages that follow feature apartment kitchens sized from almost unimaginably tiny to luxuriously large. You'll see that even a small room can feel open and nice to work in, if not exactly spacious, and you'll find aesthetics that range from quirky to retro to classic to very modern, and from informal to professional. Check out the special features, "Ten Great Details for Small Kitchens," "It's All in the Details," and "Kitchen Storage Smarts." Enjoy your perfect kitchen.

> **TIP:** A deep windowsill offers extra shelf space in a kitchen—perfect for pots of herbs, crocks of utensils, or the cookie jar.

ABOVE: Vanilla tones on the walls and cabinets (refrigerator door panels included), chrome hardware, and white marble countertops keep the atmosphere open. Glass cabinet doors reflect light, but they also display their contents, so think of what is inside your cabinets before exposing them to view.

ABOVE: Stainless-steel appliances look sleek and professional, whether commercial or conventional in scale. Note two simple luxuries here—a niche below the hood to keep essentials handy, and a built-out backsplash below the window for display or storage.

TIP: A bottom drawer freezer compartment saves wear on your back because the refrigerator, which you open more frequently, will be easier to access.

ABOVE: A big window and a certain mid-century retro charm are the chief assets of this small kitchen. With so little counter or wall space, anything in view should be decorative as well as functional; orange and bright green make this spot sizzle.

OPPOSITE: Industrial metal shelving provides sturdy, flexible storage and keeps the upper half of this kitchen more open than cabinets would. It's a nice complement to the stainless-steel refrigerator, too.

ABOVE: Stainless steel and black granite have an industrial look that's softened when mixed with warm cherry wood. The handsome bar counter appears to float, a nice touch since it's viewed from a larger living space.

OPPOSITE: A generous U-shape layout provides lots of storage and work space in a minimal area. This one is open above the base cabinets on the side with the sink, so it feels spacious as well as efficient. The breakfast bar backs up to the counter and facilitates serving and conversation.

TIP: Flooring requires a trade-off: Porcelain tiles are inexpensive and durable but hard on your feet; wood is soft to walk on but requires more maintenance.

ABOVE: It can be challenging to integrate kitchen furnishings with adjacent living spaces in a loft. In this example, the cabinets topped by a counter with a high backsplash are handsome, and large photographs replace upper cabinets (which wouldn't fit in front of the end window anyway) and provide continuity with those in the next room.

OPPOSITE: Understated design is an excellent choice when a kitchen is open to other living areas. This space couldn't be simpler, yet the white cabinets, farmhouse sink with elegant faucet, soapstone counters, and white subway tile make a lovely and detailed composition.

TIP: Glass or high-glazed ceramic backsplash tiles bounce light and add color and pattern.

RIGHT: A kitchen that's wide open to the dining area allows cooks and diners to interact. Here, a breakfast bar that can double as a buffet also provides work space, making up for counter area given over to the deep cabinets adjacent to the windows. The white cabinets are punctuated occasionally with stainless-steel cabinets, creating a sleek contrast.

TIP: Fluorescent lighting makes a kitchen look cold and austere, like an operating room. It's your home—keep the lighting warm and inviting.

LEFT: Consider creating an interior window to link kitchen and dining areas without actually merging them. This one opens above the kitchen counter, lets the cook be part of the party, and serves as a pass-through.

ABOVE: In an open floor plan, a half-height wall offers a way to define and bring light to a windowless interior kitchen. This one is tall enough to hide the counter on the kitchen side and serve as a breakfast bar or extra workstation. The counter wraps around the corner into the next room, providing a small display area for a vase of flowers.

OPPOSITE: Stainless steel, coppery hues, and black are a never-fail combination, guaranteed to produce a handsome kitchen that can swing from industrial modern to contemporary country with the appliance and cabinet style. The cabinet's curved hardware matches the handles on the refrigerator and freezer.

ABOVE, RIGHT: Wood and stainless steel combine to give this compact kitchen a sleek, modern feel. Efficiently designed, the appliances are close to the island work space. Guests can sit at the island while the host prepares dinner.

TIP: Honed stone countertops are soft to the touch and reflect less glare than polished ones.

ABOVE: An interior window fitted with shelves allows fanciful zebra-pattern wallpaper to overflow into this tiny kitchen from the dining area beyond without overwhelming. A display of clear glassware provides an uninterrupted view. The corner sink is noteworthy here.

OPPOSITE: Cabinetry with inset doors, shelves seen through glass, open storage cubes, and a tile backsplash compose a variety of grid patterns on these walls. The blue glass tiles and a slate countertop provide a restful focal point amid the mix of gleaming stainless steel and glass and the rich, honey-hued wood cabinets.

ABOVE: Attention to detail makes up for lack of space in this miniscule kitchenette. The petite basin is fitted with a tall faucet to accommodate deep pans or vases, the two-burner cooktop is flanked with a modicum of counter, the skirt requires less space to open than cabinet doors, and the colors are restful.

OPPOSITE: Good design solutions may lie hidden in quirky architectural details. Here, stepped masonry from a chimney provides graduated shelving, a charming backdrop for a tiny prep area. The curtain hides under-sink storage where a cabinet wouldn't fit, and the projecting countertop sneaks in a bit more work surface.

ABOVE: An eat-in kitchen doesn't get much better than this—French doors pour light on dining and cooking areas; the wainscoting and tiled floors remind us this is a work space; and the round pedestal table and bentwood chairs are at once visually light.

ABOVE: A display of great looking dishes makes a perfect backdrop to a table and chairs in a large kitchen. The sideboard offers handsome storage as well as a surface for serving; the open wall shelf balances lightly above it. The wire chairs and table pedestal keep the look airy.

Before and After:
Small Can Be Beautiful

Before

Depressing is hardly the word for this 1936 kitchen, which was in worse than original state. The tiny room was dark, dreary, and had virtually no counterspace. There was nowhere to sit nor room for a table—just an awkward, useless space between the range and window—and the exhaust fan with airborne cord was definitely not a plus.

After

Determined to make room for counters along both sides of the room, the new owner bravely demolished the plumbing wall and moved it back about 18 inches. This eliminated the odd space next to the radiator, created a recess for cabinets and counter, and allowed for a bench in the newly opened span below the window. The range was replaced and relocated to the opposite side of the room.

1. A small round table on wheels scoots easily for access to the bench. Its wire legs keep it from looking heavy or awkward.
2. The top of the bench is flush with the radiator cover, creating a deep windowsill.
3. An undermounted sink looks sleek and uncluttered—best of all, one swipe with a sponge sends drips and spills into it.
4. The handy raised shelf on the counter provides handsome camouflage for the original plumbing stack; there's a flue for the pipes inside the cabinets.
5. Glass-fronted upper cabinets stop short of the window to keep the space feeling open. There are narrow open shelves at their end.
6. Contemporary, adjustable track lighting can be focused where needed and looks nifty.

TEN GREAT DETAILS FOR SMALL KITCHENS

1. **Crown molding.** Molding at the wall and ceiling joint adds a polished finish and can make a room feel bigger.

2. **Cabinet doors.** Mix solid-panel and glass-front cabinet doors to create a focal point: The eye tends to sweep past solid doors and go straight to the glass-front ones.

3. **Eat-in kitchen.** In an apartment, having more than just one place to eat makes the overall habitat feel more spacious. Try to find a nook or cranny where you can squeeze in a small countertop and stools.

4. **Display space.** A glass shelf installed near the top of a window can show off a collection without blocking the light. Top cabinets with pretty bowls or vases.

5. **Task lighting.** Recessed lights beneath hanging cabinets provide vital focused illumination for working at the counters below, especially if windows are lacking.

6. **Plate rack.** This is a good storage trick for a space-deprived kitchen. It adds a great look, and you won't have to open a cabinet every time you need a plate.

7. **Deep sink.** Instead of a wide sink, opt for a deep one. You'll gain counter space and find it easier to fill pots.

8. **Colors.** Work out a color scheme by finding one thing in the kitchen that you love and then coordinate other items with it—using the same color family for all.

9. **Appliance camouflage.** Install a custom panel to conceal the dishwasher so that your small space won't be overwhelmed by a solid wall of appliances.

10. **Custom cabinets.** If your budget allows for it, have custom cabinets designed and installed—they'll make the best use of every inch of your kitchen.

IT'S ALL IN THE DETAILS

Here are eight aspects of your décor that are fairly easy to update but often overlooked. Getting them right can make the difference between a generic space and home, and transform your space from shabby to up-to-date.

1. **Hardware.** From cabinet handles and hinges to the knobs on your entry or interior doors, hardware is so functional and taken for granted that we often forget it has style. There are countless options and it's usually easy to change.

2. **Flooring and carpets.** These add color and warmth; they can also add pattern—think tile, parquet, and woven design. While replacing your flooring may be too big of an undertaking, refinishing a wood floor or installing an attached carpet are both options. Area carpets or rugs can be moved when you do.

3. **Moldings.** Architectural detail at the ready, chair rails, crown moldings, pilasters, frames, and roundels may add the elegance you covet or impose a dated look you can't abide. Depending on which, you can add them, remove them, highlight them with paint, or paint them over.

4. Countertops. It's relatively easy to replace countertops and doing so can give your kitchen (or bathroom vanity) a great face-lift even if you can't replace the cabinets.

5. Appliances. Updates are easy and only as costly as you wish. Consider surface (for both style and upkeep), cost of operating, and ambient noise, which may be surprisingly apparent in a small apartment.

6. Fixtures and fittings. Tubs, sinks—even toilets—have style, and old, chipped or scratched ones are not an enhancement to your sense of well-being. Good looking faucets and controls make a huge difference; sometimes new ones are all it takes to update an older bath or kitchen.

7. Wallcoverings. Be it paint, wallpaper, or a textile, plain is always fine, but pattern may appeal to you. If you plan to redo, consider the scale of any pattern and whether you want to add sheen or incorporate a texture. Get a sample and look at it in different types of daylight and in lamplight.

8. Window treatments. Regardless of their decorating style, most apartment dwellers need window coverings that provide privacy. Even if you eschew curtain panels or fancy swags, include opaque, adjustable shades or blinds in your decorating plan—they'll virtually disappear when raised.

KITCHEN STORAGE SMARTS

Kitchen storage should be convenient—include it as part of your overall setup, not as an afterthought. Here are things to consider.

Zone your kitchen. Assign every task and activity to a specific location. Decide which accoutrements belong in each zone and then figure out how to put them there.

Measure everything. Record the inside dimensions of cabinets, cupboards, and drawers so you can add storage devices that fit them efficiently.

Divide and conquer. Add drawer dividers; use stacking bins and wire or plastic shelves in larger cabinets. • Group same-size jars so they fit side-by-side neatly. • Be imaginative—a cutlery tray may be the perfect thing for your spices. • Use vertical dividers to separate lids, racks, and baking sheets. • It's fine to nest bowls and baking dishes as long as you can access them easily. • Screw cup hooks under shelves, or add a hanging system for stemware. • Get a rack for boxed food wraps. • Invest in stackable food storage containers—they'll keep your fridge neater.

Pullout storage works wonders. Whether drawers and sliding shelves are part of your cabinets or inserts you add, they make it easy to access the back of a storage space.

Use the wall space. Hanging storage is convenient and can be very attractive. Incorporate wire grid, rack, or bar systems for utensils and pans, many of these systems can be fitted with shallow shelves and baskets for condiments, lids, cookbooks, or even a pot of herbs.

Trash happens. Make a plan for your garbage and recyclables from the outset. Home supply stores have slide-out trash can supports you can add to your base cabinets.

Display great gear. If you have handsome copper pans or colorful mixing bowls, don't stash them away; give them a prominent place in the kitchen.

Weighty matters. Put heavy things in lower cabinets.

Be realistic. If you have a small kitchen, admit it and don't expect it to accommodate banquet equipment.

BATHROOMS

4

Sparkling, relaxing yet energizing, comfortable, private. Your list of ideal bathroom attributes might also include luxurious, romantic, airy, and easy to maintain. You may be yearning for a spa, wishing for a space big enough for a double shower, or simply want never again to see the aged tile in your classic tub and shower. Your dreams and plans may be based on purely aesthetic goals—to have a bathroom that's beautiful in a way the one you've got is not; or driven by physical conditions— deterioration caused by water or age, or a mix of both—a desire for more attractive fixtures, better lighting, or an improved layout and a need for a face-lift of paint, caulk, or ventilation system.

Because they are regularly suffused with steam, the recipients of splashes and drips, and home to damp towels, bathrooms are challenging in the best of circumstances, and thus successful bathroom design is part aesthetics and part practicality. If you live in an older building, you may have a bathroom with wonderful period charm and ample proportions that you want to preserve, yet be faced with deteriorating surfaces or fixtures and inadequate lighting. If your building is new, you may find the bathroom bland or unpleasantly cold and sterile. Unless your bath has been recently updated, it's not surprising to find it in need of anything from new paint to a complete renovation.

Whatever your goal for your bathroom, even if you are redecorating or renovating for entirely cosmetic reasons, you want to be sure the update will solve whatever problems you have with your current setup and wear well. To get off to a

OPPOSITE: A panel of small, richly and irregularly colored brown tiles set with pale grout forms a strong frame behind this wall-mounted sink and plain mirror and adds an element of verticality to the small room.

good start, consider the questions outlined in the Introduction—they'll help you evaluate whether the physical and financial challenges of altering plumbing, fixtures, and wiring are a wise undertaking for your particular situation as a renter or an owner.

Once you determine the appropriate scope for the job ahead, it's time to pull together your thoughts and ideas and plan the details. Begin by listing your goals and noting the particular challenges or problems you want to overcome. Apartment bathrooms often lack good ventilation, natural light, or adequate storage—is this the case for yours, and if so, is it feasible for you to add a window or a closet or will you need another solution to the problem? Must you exchange a pedestal sink for a vanity in order to add storage? If you are on a budget, can you justify a marble tile floor if you install it yourself—and can you realistically do so?

To answer these questions and find inspiration, look through the photos in this chapter; flag the ones that appeal to you, including images of details as well as overall design. Also clip pictures of bathrooms you like from magazines or catalogs. Be open to clever ideas for lighting, layout, or storage even if their aesthetic is not the look you are after. And to make sure you plan for efficient use of your space, read "Three Easy Steps to a Tidy Bathroom." You'll find you are well on your way to your ideal bathroom.

TIP: A light hung above and slightly in front of the mirror won't be blocked by your head or elbows.

ABOVE: Large square tiles, in two tones of terra-cotta, stripe the walls in an unusual application that provides a strong, graphic background for this bathroom. The wall-mounted sink features a small, very convenient, integral counter.

ABOVE: An imaginative designer used wave-like borders—painted around the mirror and sewn to the shower curtain—to give this bare-bones bath a splash of style, then added a tailored skirt to create under-sink storage and a simple sisal rug to complete the seaside effect.

ABOVE: A quintessential urban apartment bath—white throughout, with subway tile on the walls, tiny hexagonal tiles on the floor, and simple fixtures with chrome fittings—is updated here with a console basin, new large showerhead, and nifty laundry hamper. This design scheme is always clean and soothing.

TIP: If wall space is limited, mount towel bars on the back of the bathroom door, or buy a rack designed to hang over the top of the door.

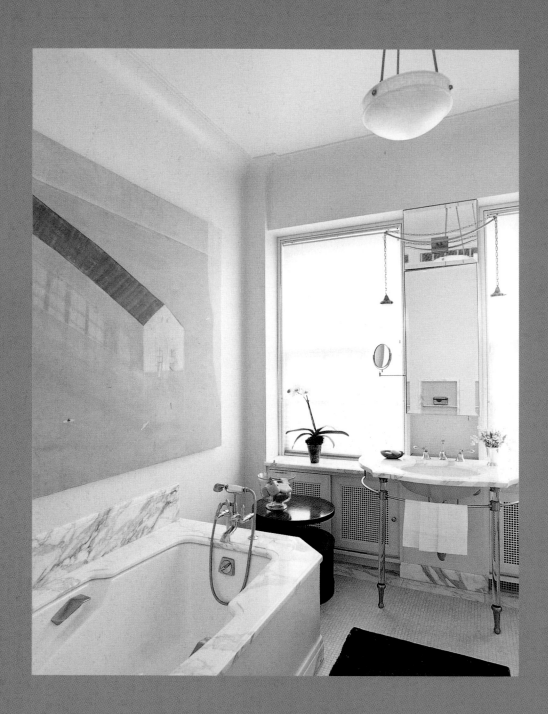

OPPOSITE: Stone tiles covering nearly every surface, the huge mirrored cabinet, and frameless glass doors on the tub shower give this bath an austere sophistication. The sink counter is striking, with the faucet and controls mounted on the backsplash and a makeup station adjacent to the basin.

ABOVE, RIGHT: This classic bath has been elegantly outfitted with handsome shower and basin controls, a neatly secured curtain pole, and a graceful, oversize sconce. The shiny, uniform wall surface and inset mirrored cabinet door make a sleek contrast to the cloth shower curtain and traditional fixtures.

TIP: Place big mirrors opposite one another to enlarge a small bathroom.

ABOVE: A random pattern of assorted glazed and unglazed two-inch tiles gives plenty of interest to this tub and shower alcove. The open wooden shelves, exotic wooden stool, and brown floor mat coordinate well with the tiles; everything else is crisply white.

TIP: A heated towel bar is a justifiable luxury, especially if your bathroom is chilly. It helps damp towels to dry, too.

ABOVE: A small, deep, soaking tub with a handheld personal shower may be just the option when space is tight. The niche built behind this one holds bath products and makes a complementary horizontal accent in the alcove, as do the large rectangular tiles.

OPPOSITE: Golden glazed walls and an interesting, counter-mounted lamp give this thoroughly modern basin alcove a warm glow. The glass basin sits atop a stone counter, and the water control is mounted on the mirror, which elegantly doubles the effect of each accoutrement.

ABOVE, RIGHT: This classic all-white bath gets a boost from the contemporary lamp on the wall above the framed mirror (which is the medicine cabinet door). Whether period or brand new, a glass shelf on metal brackets is an asset where there is neither vanity nor counter.

TIP: Splurge on a new faucet or showerhead to quickly spruce up a tired bathroom.

BELOW: There's always a pretty face in the mirror of this retro bathroom. Whimsy aside, the small, painted bureau provides needed storage and counter space and, with glass knobs, stainless-steel trim, and a top tiled to match the tiles on the walls, it feels right at home.

OPPOSITE: Frameless glass separates the shower from the rest of the bathroom without diminishing the overall space or impeding the light from the large window. There is no threshold and the stone tiled floor flows without interruption throughout. A large mirror further enhances the commodious ambiance.

ABOVE: Lovely custom woodwork creates a warm environment in this bath. The vanity is extra-deep to permit a built-out mirror with small storage cubbies up the sides; the long-arm sconce ensures that light reaches the mirror.

OPPOSITE: Here is a perfect example of how a few small details can work together to have a big impact on a room. This is a very small bathroom, but the scallop-edged curtains, monogrammed hand towel, and small vase with a single bloom make it pretty and attractive. Baskets provide much-needed storage.

OPPOSITE: A palette of springtime hues perfectly suits this unusual combination bath and dressing room with its plump cushioned seat between two bureaus, exuberant collection of shells and majolica plates, the array of seasonal flowers, and pretty striped shower curtain.

ABOVE: If you've space in your bathroom to do your nails, read to a soaking mate (or need an inviolable retreat), you might as well be seated in stylish comfort. This satin-covered armchair is plenty cozy and doubles as a good interim spot for towels, clothing, etc.

THREE EASY STEPS TO A TIDY BATHROOM

Begin your bathroom organizing with a reality check: How many people share the room? What must you store there? And what is optional? Are there built-in cupboards, or is freestanding storage an option?

1. **Find another home for these:** Towels and linens—damp is the enemy of textiles, so if possible, keep only towels currently in use in your bathroom. • Bulk paper goods—if you have lots of closet space in you bathroom, fine, but otherwise, put paper products elsewhere or buy in smaller quantities. • Cleaning supplies—sure, it's convenient to have them handy, but chemicals and mops don't mix with toiletries.

2. **Help yourself to keep things tidy.** Towel bars provide better drying surface than rings. • Add-on cupboard organizers such as wire shelves, small divided bins, and caddies keep items separated and accessible and hold bottles upright. • Add a medicine cabinet if none is there; put a lock on it to prevent children from playing with the contents. • Stacking bins with drawers don't take much floor space and require no installation. • Hanging shelf units often include drawers, hooks, or a towel bar. • Slide an étagère with open or closed storage over your toilet. • Keep wastebaskets small and empty them often. • Use a shower caddy—chrome wears better than coated wire.

3. **Good design helps banish clutter.** Even if you are outfitting a small bath on a low budget, it makes sense to keep an aesthetic eye on your organizing. If your bathroom looks attractive, you'll be more likely to keep it tidy; a mishmash of bins and baskets that never looks neat will soon overflow; towels and robes that clash with the walls don't ask for respect. Accessories are easy to come by in catalogs and home stores, so survey the options and make a plan that looks good and solves your storage challenge.

5

BEDROOMS

Serene, secluded, comfortable, personal. Your ideal bedroom might also be airy, cozy, romantic, capacious, or spare. No matter its size or style, a bedroom should be a refuge, a private place designed to suit your needs and tastes. Sleep is probably its principal use, but as you plan its décor, think of what else you use your bedroom for—dressing room, office, library, craft studio—and accommodate whatever this might be. However you set it up, make sure there is good reading light—next to an easy chair, at the bedside, or both.

You may be blessed with a large and gracious bedroom or find yourself learning to love one that is tiny. If you live in a studio apartment, you lack the luxury of separation from the rest of your home and must either camouflage your bed or flaunt it. Whatever your situation, as an apartment dweller, privacy and quiet are probably issues for you, and closet space is likely one, too. Where there are nearby neighbors' windows or pedestrians, window treatments are a must; if there is ambient street light at night, you want light-blocking coverage even if your location is removed from straying eyes. Soundproofing, whether structural or added with carpets and draperies, will muffle sounds from neighboring quarters and the street—and tone down music, conversation, or feet pattering in other rooms of your own home. If closet space is tight, an armoire or bureau can supplement storage; depending on

OPPOSITE: A palette of saturated pastels in a mix of warm and cool hues gives a sophisticated edge to this bedroom. Although the color choices are pink, lavender, and pale blue, the modern furnishings and tailored linens swing the décor away from little-girl sweet to provide a softly sleek ambiance.

your situation and the look you wish to live with, closet organizing systems or built-in cupboards could be better solutions.

The style you choose for your bedroom is up to you: The décor can be as eccentric, overblown, or minimalist as you like. However, if you do spend a lot of waking time in the room, you may prefer a tailored look that makes you feel alert or professional to something romantic or sweet with a profusion of linens or distracting accessories. In a studio apartment it often makes sense to consider the "bedroom" furnishings as living room pieces, with a sofa bed, or a daybed dressed to be a sofa, and a chest of drawers that complements your other "public" accessories.

As you begin to pull your ideas together, think over the questions in the Introduction—they'll help you assess the nature of the work ahead, and, especially if you are contemplating structural changes, they'll remind you to evaluate the undertaking for your situation as a renter or owner. Jot down your goals for your bedroom—are there problems you wish to solve or is your chief interest a cosmetic makeover? Look through the photos in this chapter and pick out those that appeal to you; be sure to flag any that provide solutions to challenges you face even if the décor isn't what you have in mind. Read the special features: "Set Up a Closet That Works," "Why Textiles Matter," and "White-on-White." Refine your plan, put it in motion, and look forward to sweet dreams.

OPPOSITE: Brightly colored accessories enliven a decorating scheme, especially when set against lots of white. Here the sharp contrast of hot orange against white is beautifully balanced by a cool blue kimono sprayed with orange flowers.

ABOVE: A mix of sliding and swinging translucent glass panels makes an adjustable barrier between this bedroom and living room, allowing light and air to circulate and providing privacy when desired. Note the large mirror that balances the window on the opposite side of the bed and visually opens the space still further.

OPPOSITE: While the rough brick floor and sloped ceiling distinguish this space from the everyday studio, the use of the floor-to-ceiling sheer curtain to separate public and private areas without diminishing the space or light is a simple idea that anyone who lives in one room can borrow.

ABOVE: The clean lines of tailored upholstery and soft Roman shades combine with creamy tones and matched accessories to create a formal bedroom that invites conversation, reflection, and relaxation. The twin floor lamps and the symmetry of the plates on the wall enhance the tailored atmosphere.

OPPOSITE: In the same room as above, the bed is positioned away from the street and dressed to match the loveseat and window shades. The upholstered headboard and matching nightstands complete the ensemble of furnishings.

OPPOSITE: Reflected here in a huge framed mirror, the full-length curtains covering the wall on each side of the window make a cocoon-like backdrop for the bed and give the illusion of additional windows behind them.

ABOVE: Sleek furnishings, a mix of seascape colors, and a variety of materials keep this bedroom calm and quiet. The iridescent silk that upholsters the walls changes under differing light conditions, going from blue to green with a subtle movement like sunshine and shadow playing on ocean waves.

ABOVE: While white-on-white has been used to keep this tiny room looking as large as possible, textured details—the bed canopy, pleated lampshades, and simple upholstered headboard—keep it interesting. Red accents add dash while the brass canopy frame and mismatched antique wooden tables stand in silhouette against the walls.

ABOVE: There's barely room to walk between this bed and the chair tucked under the window, yet having a private spot in which to read, write, or knit gives a bedroom twice its usual value—even at the price of a squeeze.

TIP: If you layer a space with color, texture, and an array of styles, your décor choices will have a much longer life.

ABOVE: A bookshelf niche next to the bed, and chairs in front of the large window allow this room to double as a small library. The furnishings—formal landscape, tailored linens, fur throw, classic pleated draperies, and whimsical pendant light—indicate an occupant with eclectic tastes.

ABOVE: In a small apartment, it's important to have furniture that can serve more than one function. The white table works as a nightstand, desk, and dining table. The swinging-arm lamp provides illumination for reading in bed as well as task lighting for working at the table. The beautiful sleigh bed is the star of the room, while the curtains are simple and tailored so as not to overwhelm the small space.

ABOVE: This sleeping alcove is set off by bright red, floor-to-ceiling curtains: On the left the curtains divide the bed from living space, on the right they flank a window, and at the head of the bed they open to reveal a built-in bookcase—making work a bed position that would be otherwise awkward and providing an intimate ambiance overall.

ABOVE: A ceiling-mounted pole allows this alcove to be curtained off from the adjacent living room. The white, ring-topped curtains match those at the far window, ensuring that the décor is unified at all times, from all angles.

OPPOSITE: A panel of gathered, sheer white fabric suspended from a ring hung high above the bed makes a tent-like enclosure. Sunlight flooding through the window at the head of the bed creates an ethereal mood.

TIP: A neutral palette helps create a serene, sophisticated environment.

ABOVE: These framed translucent panels make the best of a dearth of closets: angled rods projecting from the wall behind them hold clothes. Advantage: The size of the room appears undiminished and transforms your wardrobe into a framed work of art.

OPPOSITE: Here, a curved wall screens a bed alcove. The cool blue arc is sculptural and sits lightly in the white space, maintaining the easy flow of light, air, and traffic while offering some privacy.

ABOVE: Brick walls provide a softly patterned textured backdrop that makes a surprising complement to this eclectic collection of Asian and contemporary furnishings. The key to finding things that work? Each piece must be visually strong enough not to be swallowed by the walls. In addition, the rug mutes the bold contrast of the dark floor.

RIGHT: An array of colorful patterned pillowcases and accessories provides visual texture in this simple white bedroom. Aside from the red and blue hues, these items were chosen not necessarily because they "go together," but because they create an overall pleasing and eclectic atmosphere.

ABOVE: Go for dark walls to make a sleeping space restful, something to consider if ambient city lights filter into your bedroom. Here, deep chocolate makes a fitting background for tailored linens, spare furnishings, and arresting graphics.

OPPOSITE: Dark walls bring intimacy to this mezzanine sleeping area, which, being open to the stairs and floor below on one side, could feel rather exposed. The honey-colored ceiling, floor, and throw and the sepia-tone prints in gold frames dispel any sense that the dark is closing in on you.

ABOVE: Black and white is satisfyingly graphic—make it symmetrical and the effect is especially crisp, clean, and orderly. Note here the upholstered headboard that extends behind the bedside chests in a modern take on wainscoting and also the grace note of the yellow lampshades.

RIGHT: The very shiny black floor provides contrast and a needed visual anchor in the mezzanine bedroom in this dramatic white loft. There's a transparent half-wall along the edge for unobtrusive safety and pocket doors that pull out for privacy.

ABOVE: A symmetrical display of artwork helps to balance a large piece of furniture like a bureau, adding height without mass and keeping the bureau from looking lonely. Here, framed botanicals sit gently against the floral wallpaper. The stacked vintage suitcases are a whimsical touch and provide additional storage.

ABOVE: The pretty mirror centered over this bureau is the hub for a display of framed botanicals. Placed opposite a window to reflect the cityscape, it gives the illusion of a portal through the interior wall.

ABOVE: A heavy metal fire door is a relic from this building's days as an industrial space. Now it adds architectural interest to a serene white bedroom. An old-fashioned metal bed frame echoes the metal door, while the white bed linens and white upholstered daybed soften the industrial atmosphere.

OPPOSITE: A custom-built platform bed sets the tone in this minimalist bedroom. The translucent sliding door closes the sleeping area off from the rest of the loft. Note the wavy ceiling—it provides a few soft curves in the rectilinear space.

ABOVE: This tall wooden folding screen, composed of square lattice panels, does more than take the place of a headboard. It's intriguing, adds texture, provides focus, takes up no space, requires little or no installation, and is portable—all excellent qualities for enhancing a bedroom that's small and architecturally unadorned.

BELOW: Built-in windowsill-height cabinets and a tall headboard bring architectural interest to a room that's otherwise plain. These cabinets provide a one-piece alternative to bureau, display shelves, and nightstand with no decision needed as to how best arrange them.

RIGHT: Canopied and elaborately turned, this four-poster frame invites sweet dreams in a room-within-a-room. It's big, but that's the point, especially since it must hold its own against bold patterns on the walls and upholstery.

OPPOSITE: A delicate, metal four-poster frame, dressed with neither canopy nor hangings, provides a sense of enclosure yet enjoys all the light and air present in the room, a great device in a room like this one, with its high ceilings and tall windows.

TIP: Soft layers are romantic: Add more pillows, lace, and throws if that's the look you're after.

ABOVE: Very simple furnishings, well chosen and well placed, make the most of this small bedroom, whose best assets are the windows on adjacent walls. A thoughtful use of color on one wall keeps the space interesting, enhancing the calm room with its uncomplicated furniture and few accessories.

TIP: For a creative accent in an all-white modern room, paint just one wall a color—it will recede and add dimension to the room.

OPPOSITE: Here's a stylish, discreet (and inexpensive) substitute for nightstands: a shelf extending on each side of the bed to the adjacent wall. To keep this small room as open as possible, walls, shelves, upholstered headboard, and linens all are white; the blue throw adds a soft contrast.

ABOVE: Here, a great use of color and thoughtful composition rescue the requisite bed, side tables, lamps, and blank wall from boredom. The arrangement is a good reminder that a balanced design need not be perfectly symmetrical.

OPPOSITE: Little more than a hallway, this sleeping area connects the foyer and living area in a small studio apartment. The furniture, while simple, is dressy, decorative, and not overtly "bedroomy." The high headboard and footboard on the bed provide a sense of enclosure and privacy—nice since the foot is adjacent to the living area.

TIP: A daybed with high headboard and footboard becomes a room within a room—perfect for a studio apartment.

ABOVE: Despite the visual perfection of the wardrobe arrangement, this closet nonetheless offers some excellent tips: Install the pole no higher than needed for your longest garment, then add shelves above it for folded items and storage boxes. A good paint job will encourage you to keep things tidy.

LEFT: It goes without saying that closets rarely are plentiful enough. Here, a plain, shoulder-high armoire—much less fussy than a period wardrobe—makes up for lack of built-in storage and provides display space.

ABOVE: Handsome as well as clever, this custom-built combination headboard and wall unit perfectly complements the modern chairs and table. Doors on the upper cabinets fold down to double as bedside tables; the center section is covered with fabric that harmonizes with the bed linens.

ABOVE: A sconce mounted just above pillow-height is a perfect source of bedtime reading light that can't be knocked over by elbow or cat. One with an adjustable arm like this is a plus. Sconces do require installation by an electrically savvy person—if retro-fitting, remember this before purchasing.

TIP: If you love to read in bed, a solid headboard provides a good way to prop up the pillows so you can lean against them.

OPPOSITE: This large round mirror, set in an elliptical frame and centered above the bed, reflects ambient light. Absent anyone crossing the foot of the bed, it shows the opposite, blank, wall, appearing transparent and giving the sculptural frame its due. Note the extended upholstered headboard and interesting chenille bedcover.

ABOVE: A tall mirror next to this bed frames a reflection of the hall and living room like a large, graphic painting—a fitting complement to the bold polka dot rug and the intense blue panel filling the frame at the head of the bed.

Before and After:
Bold Strokes on a Small Scale

Before

This tiny room comprises almost all the space in a diminutive walk-up apartment and must serve for living, dining, and sleeping. A regimented arrangement of white furnishings with neutral accents kept the space as open as possible, but was bland and looked cluttered rather than composed. Off-center windows added to the challenge.

After

The owner felt she might as well flaunt what she didn't have, and opted to make the small space lively. Possessing an excellent eye for design, she looked for one bold gesture that would transform her room, and decided to exploit her love of red by using it everywhere—as an accent—to unite her jumbled furnishings. The result is an individual décor with unmistakable passion and new comfort.

1. A single pair of curtains spans the end wall—they minimize the off-center focus, take less space than two pairs, and are trimmed with red ribbon.
2. The armoire has been moved across the room for a more comfortable fit.
3. Thick cushions have transformed the radiator covers into window seats—a great way to accommodate guests in a room where there's barely space for a single easy chair.
4. A shocking pink Parsons table doubles for desk and dining. The glossy scarlet lamp shade atop a swirling glass base provides light.
5. Red-and-white textiles in assorted patterns and small amounts enliven various furnishings—plaid on the ottoman, ticking stripe on the headboard and for the armoire curtains, toile for a bench and chair.

Before and After:
Good-bye to Gloom

Before
The symmetry of paired casement windows at one end of this bedroom was spoiled by an air conditioner and their proportions distorted by the remnant of a cornice that must have topped curtains at one time (the damask laid on the cross grain could never have been an asset). Tattered window shades and worn wallpaper completed the bleak décor.

After
The windows assumed their rightful proportions among pilasters and soffits as soon as the cornice was removed. White paint gives a clean, serene background and the windows, now dressed with discreet white shades, are free to flood the room with daylight.

1. Matched easy chairs in front of the windows take advantage of the room's length as well as its light; there is plenty of space for a sitting area.
2. A simple, custom-made headboard, upholstered in soft chenille, centers the bed on the plain wall.
3. A small, wall-mounted lamp with a flexible arm provides good reading light; its switches are within arm's reach, so there's no need to leave the bed to turn them off.
4. Paired, low bedside tables are generously sized to hold books, flowers, water, coffee, or whatever accoutrements are needed.
5. The jazzy overhead fan keeps the air circulating in all seasons.

SET UP A CLOSET THAT WORKS

Closets that are well outfitted hold a lot more than you expect. So shop for your closet—there are many good organizing systems, some readymade, some made-to-measure. And check out the clothing displays in boutiques. You'll find good ideas for fitting lots of garments in a small space.

Analyze your needs and then set up your space. The person who always dresses in jeans and tees has very different needs than the person who frequents the ballroom every weekend. Measure the space you need to store different kinds of garments. Consider: Cubbyhole storage keeps everything in view and you don't need space for yourself to stand while you pull out a drawer.   Deep drawers may be good for handbags, but for clothing they're an invitation to rummage. Save them for pillows and towels.   Store shirts folded in a bureau if you're short of hanging space.   Use tiered rods for short garments (fold trousers over their hangers); allocate only the space you really need for longer dresses and coats. It's easier to find what you want if you separate your clothing by the occasion for which it's suited (business, casual, or evening) as well as by type (jackets, pants, or skirts). Take advantage of tall ceilings with high shelves for infrequently used items.

Make it easy to keep things clean and safe. Invest in zippered bags to keep out-of-season clothes dust-free. • Use the right kind of hanger in the right size to support each garment. • Keep shoes in bags, boxes, or racks so you can vacuum the floor. • Add a shelf or small table to hold jewelry or the contents of your pocket while you dress.

Use your dressing room. Install a full-length mirror in or near your closet so you don't have to trek to the bathroom to check out your outfit. • Install hooks so you can organize an outfit before putting it on or packing it. • If your closet is large, set up an iron.

WHY TEXTILES MATTER

Textiles add dimension, texture, grace, color, and pattern. They can filter light or block it altogether. They soften floors, shed or absorb water, warm beds, and mask the undesirable. They're variously durable or ephemeral, precious or disposable. Available in endless variety, they're simply invaluable as components of your décor. Choose them thoughtfully, balancing style, durability, and budget, and put them to good use.

1. **Upholstery and slipcovers:** Look for durable fabrics that feel good against your skin. Pets, children, sunlight, and spills all take a toll on fabric. Inexpensive furniture does not warrant a costly covering; good furniture is worth covering well.

2. **Rugs and carpets:** They may be flat weave or pile, patterned or plain. They come doormat to room size; use them to accent or anchor accordingly.

3. **Window treatments:** Fabric type and construction style go hand-in-hand to create formal or casual window fashions. Look in books and magazines for ideas you'd like to live with. Catalogs and home centers offer a wide variety of both ready-made and semi-custom choices. Make sure you account for your privacy needs when planning.

4. **Bed coverings:** Sheets, shams, blankets, quilts, duvet covers, throws, bed skirts and hangings—stylish options abound; custom fabrication is an option if you've something specific in mind.

5. **Kitchen accessories:** Dish towels, aprons, potholders, place mats—choose styles that coordinate with your overall kitchen décor, but bear in mind the heavy use these items get and make sure they are washable.

6. **Bath linens:** Good ones last for years, so let yourself splurge a bit. Be sure to include hand towels for guests in your collection.

7. **Dining linens:** Be sure to have a basic white tablecloth, and consider assembling a collection of both formal and casual tablecloths and napkins. Make sure you know your table size when shopping. Stain-resistant finishes are worth considering.

8. **Decorative accessories:** Throw pillows, afghans and throws, table runners and toppers—these are small items that can be changed easily and add character to your furnishings. And if you're a textile lover, you'll include ethnic weavings, samplers, art quilts, and similar treasures to display as part of your décor.

WHITE-ON-WHITE

Serene, elegant, pristine, cold, feminine, fresh, streamlined, summery, wintery, modern, or sophisticated—white is a chameleon color that suits many decorating tastes. When thoughtfully composed, an all-white décor can be many things—just not noisy or boring. Here are tips for making all-white work.

1. Pure it isn't. White needn't be limited to a single hue. Ecru, ivory, beige, straw, dove, palest blush, blue, and green tints, light natural wood tones, and antiqued and silvery metals all have a legitimate place in white-on-white décor.

2. Mix textures. Combine sheers, nubby chenille, laces, airy mohair, matelassé, smooth percale, and muslin.

3. Find nuance in layers. Tone-on-tone effects come from peeling paint, light passing through sheer fabrics on windows or furniture, a layer of lace over a solid cloth, mirrored reflections, walls painted with a ragged, striée, or pickled technique, and piles of pillows on a bed.

4. **Shadow is another kind of white.** Use white furnishings with sculptural details that cast, and catch, shadows: metal beds with ornamental fittings, woven wicker, painted pieces with carved moldings, ceramics with raised details, knobs and handles, ruffled curtains or slipcovers with gathered skirts or sashes tied in bows, and crocheted throws. Arrange white crockery in a white open cupboard.

5. **Let the sun shine in.** Natural daylight adds warmth. Both sunlight and moonlight make architecture and furnishings cast shadows, which add character.

6. **Simple or complex as befits the style.** Stick with the furnishings appropriate to your décor: Don't add ruffles to a modern interior just because the window treatment is white; don't force chrome chairs into a Victorian dining room that's decked in muslin and lace.

7. **Exploit the cleanness.** An all-white décor is always refreshing in a bathroom and makes a kitchen look wholesome and efficient. Your surface choices—matte or glazed tile, stainless steel or enamel appliances, polished marble or honed limestone, paint, wallpaper, polished or whitewashed wood—will refine the mood and swing it from clinical to sophisticated.

LIBRARIES, OFFICES, AND ENTRYWAYS 6

Exquisite extra or essential element—anyone would covet an apartment that includes a foyer or a room that can be dedicated to a library or office. If yours does not, you can create space within another room to satisfy your need for a place to drop your hat, store your books, or situate the desk. Large or small, such spaces should be designed to look great and facilitate the way you use them.

A foyer offers an immediate welcome in your home; if your apartment has a substantial entry hall, make the most of it. If not, even a small corner or hallway can be made inviting—a gloomy entry doesn't herald a warm home. Provide soft lighting, a place to put the mail and your handbag or briefcase, and decorate the space in a style that introduces the rest of your apartment.

Libraries and office space are luxuries that some of us can't do without. If you fall into this group, you'll either choose an apartment because it provides the necessary space, or you'll find a way to accommodate your bookshelves or desk (or both) in your living or dining room, in your bedroom, or even in a hall closet.

Perhaps you are planning a major renovation, and if so, you can create the spaces you need. Maybe you live in a loft where your foyer is simply the wall next to the entry door, and freestanding cupboards or shelves establish your library, or sliding

OPPOSITE: Grommeted canvas panels provide an informal background (and grand Roman shades) for the light-filled office in this garden apartment. The panels, along with the area rug, the painting, and the freestanding shelves, are aesthetically appealing options for furnishing quarters that don't warrant physical repairs or built-in décor.

237

panels create an office zone. If your quarters are more conventional, your plans will depend on how much space you can designate for these specific functions.

Apartment foyers usually lack windows, and office and library space is frequently carved from a passageway or tucked into a closet; both situations are plagued by a lack of natural light and fresh air. Whatever your situation, your needs are probably quite personal, so assess them honestly: Is your foyer really a mudroom? Or will it be your art gallery? Must your desk be behind doors? Will you need a ladder because your bookshelves stretch to the ceiling? How many people use the space? Can you afford custom-made or will you opt for furnishings from a home store or catalog? What are your requirements for wiring, cable and phone connections, and storage? If your space is to be multipurpose, what is the best overall aesthetic? How can you separate or combine the needed components?

Look through the photos in this chapter for good ideas and great design for foyers, library spaces, and offices. Go shopping to see the variety of furnishings available. Measure your space so you can ground your dreams in reality. Whatever your needs, begin your planning by giving some thought to the questions set out in the Introduction. They'll help you determine the scope of your project and whether it makes sense for you as a renter or owner. Read the special feature "Clutter Control" for ways to impose order on the contents of your space. Pull together your ideas, make a plan, and put it to work.

TIP: Accessorize your office with things that are meaningful to you—you'll enjoy it more and it will mesh nicely with the rest of your apartment.

OPPOSITE: Two steps up and sliding translucent panels set the home office apart in this spacious apartment. Note the counter-height perimeter shelves for extra work or storage space, the interior window that connects to the kitchen beyond, and the beautiful, bordered parquet floor.

TIP: You'll never be wrong to embellish your entryway with a vase of fresh flowers. Or, if you have natural light, use a large potted plant.

RIGHT: Vivid yellow splashes happily over these walls, bringing sunshine to a small, windowless foyer. The bold painting is balanced and visually anchored by a graceful painted side table, which is large enough to hold a few accessories but not so large you can't easily walk past it.

ABOVE: Quirky spots like this small landing can provide just the space required for a collection of favorite volumes and a comfortable chair. It makes sense to devote precious floor space to bookshelves when there isn't enough area for a real room anyway, and the cozy décor invites a good read.

TIP: Choose picture frames thoughtfully. The right one will complement your décor and the artwork, but the wrong one could overwhelm the art or fail to accentuate it.

ABOVE: A plastered niche is the focal point in this expanse of brick and home to a chest of drawers and artwork. Who cares that the loft's intercom, fuse box, and electric conduits are exposed next to it?

ABOVE: An architectural niche provides an empty frame begging to be filled. This one is just deep enough to hold a small sideboard and sports a tight arrangement of brightly framed graphics.

ABOVE: An awkward angle is here put to good use housing a small bookcase, keeping it out of the way but handy to the nearby worktable. A collection of small photo portraits is a bit of whimsy tacked to the wall above.

ABOVE: The composition of modules surrounding the doorway between the dining and living rooms provides open and closed storage and display space in this apartment. The unit is attractive, efficient, requires only a moderate area relative to its capacity, and extends neatly into the small, adjacent hallway.

OPPOSITE: A wall of shelves built floor-to-peak into the gable end of this room creates recessed doorways and lots of book space. White paint keeps the overall effect airy even though there's plenty on display. Somewhere a ladder awaits the call to fetch objects on the high shelves.

RIGHT: A classic library table placed in the middle of this small room leaves all the walls clear for book storage and enables someone seated there to face the windows. Two floor lamps and one on the desk make the space bright at any hour.

LEFT: A compact office was constructed in this corridor. The desk is recessed between a bank of cabinets and a high wall, and modular shelves and drawers were placed on the opposite wall. This one is open to receive ambient light from the windows in the adjacent room, yet feels private even though it has no doors.

OPPOSITE: A wide closet fitted with shelves, a counter, and a file cabinet make a neat guestroom office that disappears behind bifold doors when company comes to stay. The wood-paneled interior of this one makes it feel professional and permanent—not makeshift.

ABOVE: In small quarters, pushing a table against the sofa back may be the best way to build an office. Your work space will still be very public; this one addresses the home-and-office challenge with a neat array of understated desk accessories and a trio of potted herbs.

OPPOSITE: Sometimes the back of a mezzanine or stairwell railing offers just the right amount of space for a small desk. A setup like this may be best for people who live alone or who work when no one else is home.

ABOVE: Lots of small containers keep this tabletop desk organized despite a lack of drawers. The pretty lamp gives a soft, personal touch—perfect for a home office that doesn't want to be corporate.

OPPOSITE: A stack of books adds height to this low end table to keep the phone within easy reach.

ABOVE: A small desk with light, streamlined proportions works for correspondence and doesn't take much space. The two-tiered top of this table provides a storage platform or a home for the keyboard without the bulky appearance of drawers.

ABOVE: When space is tight, place a long, narrow table against the wall to do double duty as desk and sideboard; add an attractive lamp that suits both roles. Bins tucked below this table keep books or papers out of the way but within reach.

TIP: If you have no other space available, let your dining table double as a desk; a low-hanging light will provide the best illumination.

ABOVE: Ornate Asian cabinets provide a focal point to this small office under a sloping ceiling. The contemporary chairs and desk echo the colors found on the cabinets. Framed photos and stacks of books and periodicals fill the wall space—this room is personal and inviting.

OPPOSITE: It doesn't take much space to make a home office. Here, a table covered with a striped cloth serves as a desk, a standard-issue corkboard provides a place to pin up photos, postcards, and other mementos, a computer does the work, and a funky lamp sheds light on the occupant and other accessories.

Before and After:
Step Through a Gracious Entry

Before

An awkward step and graceless metal railing were unwelcoming and blocked the flow of traffic between this foyer and the adjacent large living room. Drab wallpaper and beadboard wainscoting made the interior room gloomy and were poor companions to the original Art Deco border hiding under the aged finish on the parquet floor.

After

With the railing, wainscoting, and wallpaper gone, and the step now spanning the full width of the opening, the transition between the foyer and living space is gracious and seamless even though a dining area now backs onto the step. White paint on walls and ceilings in both spaces make each seem a logical, inviting extension of the other.

1 The new step—a wide maple slab—appears to float across the opening. It is supported on conical feet installed tip-down and inset far enough under the step to be nearly invisible.

2 In the foyer, the owner opted for a cabinet that could hide running shoes and serve as a bench for donning them. It conceals shopping totes and other necessaries as well.

3 Cleaned to highlight its original pattern, the parquet floor is a glorious accent to the apartment's modern furnishings.

4 A wall of custom-built bookshelves was artfully tucked next to the structural pilaster that divides the spaces.

CLUTTER CONTROL

To some, clutter is anything that does not enhance your life on a regular basis. To others, it's anything, no matter how much we love it, that lands inappropriately on the kitchen table. Here are some tips for keeping both types in check.

1. **Use the walls.** Horizontally, with floating shelves to hold photos or books over desk, credenza, or buffet. Vertically, with shelves extending nearly to the ceiling to display collections or house your library or CD collection.

2. **Hideaway.** If it isn't attractive, conceal it. Opt for bookcases with doors and occasional tables with drawers.

3. **Color coordinate.** Harmonize spaces by choosing accessories with a shared palette; this helps both small accoutrements, like disc or pencil caddies, and larger ones, like picture frames or cushions and throws, to create a neat look when grouped.

4. **Love it or leave it.** Require your possessions to justify themselves: If you neither love it nor use it, toss it.

5. **Double duty.** Choose furniture that multitasks—an ottoman to double as seating and occasional table (and ideally as storage, too), a coffee table with a shelf for magazines, or a cupboard that can be topped with your collection of pitchers or bowls.

6. **Discard with discipline.** Put junk mail through the shredder or into the recycling bin as soon as it arrives. Three days is it for newspapers, and magazines go when the next edition arrives.

7. **Invite tidiness.** Provide a basket for the mail, a bowl for keys, a tray for wet boots, and a rack for hats—whatever it takes to fight the in-the-door-drop-it syndrome.

8. **Invest in order.** Purchase whatever organizing supplies are right for you—from hanging folders for your file cabinet, to drawer dividers, to magazine bins, and cardboard storage bins. If they won't be hidden, buy attractive items. Label them, if appropriate, so that you'll easily know what's inside.

9. **Display and enjoy it.** Forget stuffing your hat collection into the closet or your wooden spoons into the utensil drawer. Find a distinctive rack for the former and an appealing jug for the latter and declare them part of the decor.

PHOTOGRAPHY CREDITS

Page 2: Peter Margonelli • Page 3: Peter Margonelli • Page 6: René Stoeltie • Page 8: Thibault Jeanson • Page 10: Victoria Pearson • Page 13: Victoria Pearson • Page 14: © Fernando Bengoechea/Beateworks/Corbis • Page 15: © Fernando Bengoechea/Beateworks/Corbis • Page 16: Jonn Coolidge • Page 17: Jonn Coolidge • Page 18: Eric Roth • Page 19: Eric Roth • Page 20: Tim Beddow • Page 21: Tim Beddow • Page 23: Tria Giovan • Page 25: Tria Giovan • Page 26 (left): Eric Piasecki • Page 26 (right): Eric Piasecki • Page 27: Eric Piasecki • Page 28: © Fernando Bengoechea/Beateworks/Corbis • Page 29: © Fernando Bengoechea/Beateworks/Corbis • Page 30: Roger Davies • Page 31: Roger Davies • Page 32: Vicente Wolf • Page 34: Dominique Vorillon • Page 35: Dominique Vorillon • Page 36: Oberto Gili • Page 38: Oberto Gili • Page 39: Oberto Gili • Page 40: Eric Piasecki • Page 41: Eric Piasecki • Page 42: Mick Hales • Page 43: Mick Hales • Page 44: Tim Street-Porter • Page 45: Tim Street-Porter • Page 46: Eric Roth • Page 47: Tara Striano • Page 48: Eric Piasecki • Page 49: © istockphoto/Meliden • Page 50: Peter Margonelli • Page 51: Peter Margonelli • Page 52: © Fernando Bengoechea/Beateworks/Corbis • Page 53: Eric Roth • Page 54: Peter Murdock • Page 56: John M. Hall • Page 58: Eric Piasecki • Page 59: Eric Piasecki • Page 60: Eric Piasecki • Page 61: Eric Piasecki • Page 62: © Fernando Bengoechea/Beateworks/Corbis • Page 63: © Fernando Bengoechea/Beateworks/Corbis • Page 64: Dana Gallagher • Page 65 (left): Jonn Coolidge • Page 65 (right): Jonn Coolidge • Page 66: Roger Davies • Page 67: Peter Margonelli • Page 68: Jonn Coolidge • Page 69: Jonn Coolidge • Page 70: Luke White • Page 71: Tria Giovan • Page 72: Richard Bryant/Arcaid – Designed by Calvin Tsao and Zack McKown • Page 73: Oberto Gili • Page 74: Thibault Jeanson • Page 75: Thibault Jeanson • Page 76: Antoine Bootz • Page 77: Gaby Zimmermann • Page 78: Dominique Vorillon • Page 79: Dominique Vorillon • Page 80: Luke White • Page 81: David Phelps • Page 82: William Waldron • Page 83: Joshua McHugh • Page 85: © Fernando Bengoechea/Beateworks/Corbis • Page 86: Thibault Jeanson • Page 87: Jonn Coolidge • Page 88: Jonn Coolidge • Page 89: Rene Stoeltie • Page 90: Peter Margonelli • Page 91: Peter Margonelli • Page 92: Paul Whicheloe • Page 93: Paul Whicheloe • Page 94: Peter Margonelli • Page 95: Eric Piasecki • Page 96: Tara Striano • Page 97: Tara Striano • Page 104: Roger Davies • Page 107: © istockphoto/J. Horrocks • Page 108: © Fernando Bengoechea/Beateworks/Corbis • Page 109: Tria Giovan • Page 110: Peter Margonelli • Page 111: Tria Giovan • Page 112: Antoine Bootz • Page 113: Eric Roth • Page 114: Peter Murdock • Page 115: Laura Resen • Page 116: Jonn Coolidge • Page 117: Paul Whicheloe • Page 118: Vicente Wolf • Page 120: William Waldron • Page 121: Tara Striano • Page 122: Tria Giovan • Page 123: Tim Beddow • Page 124: © Fernando

Bengoechea/Beateworks/Corbis • Page 125: Eric Roth • Page 126: Eric Piasecki • Page 127: Eric Piasecki • Page 132: Tria Giovan • Page 135 (left): Tria Giovan • Page 135 (right): Tria Giovan • Page 136: Victoria Pearson • Page 137: Carlos Domenech • Page 138: Mick Hales • Page 139: Mick Hales • Page 140: Christopher Irion • Page 141: Dana Gallagher • Page 143: Vicente Wolf • Page 144: Peter Margonelli • Page 145: Peter Murdock • Page 146: © Fernando Bengoechea/Beateworks/Corbis • Page 147: © istockphoto/Joe Brandt • Page 148: Eric Piasecki • Page 149: © Fernando Bengoechea/Beateworks/Corbis • Page 150: Jan Tham • Page 151: Tim Street-Porter • Page 152: Oberto Gili • Page 153: Antoine Bootz • Page 154: Tara Striano • Page 155: Tara Striano • Page 162: Mick Hales • Page 165: Peter Murdock • Page 166: William Waldron • Page 167: © Fernando Bengoechea/Beateworks/Corbis • Page 168: Oberto Gili • Page 169: Peter Murdock • Page 170: Peter Margonelli • Page 171: © Fernando Bengoechea/Beateworks/Corbis • Page 172: Dominique Vorillon • Page 173: Luke White • Page 174: Peter Margonelli • Page 175: Peter Margonelli • Page 176: Victoria Pearson • Page 177: Vicente Wolf • Page 178: Tim Street-Porter • Page 179: © Fernando Bengoechea/ Beateworks/Corbis • Page 180: © Fernando Bengoechea/Beateworks/Corbis • Page 181: © Fernando Bengoechea/Beateworks/Corbis • Page 184: Tim Beddow • Page 187: Victoria Pearson • Page 188: Jan Tham • Page 189: Paul Whicheloe • Page 190: Tria Giovan • Page 191: Tria Giovan • Page 192: Vicente Wolf • Page 193: Vicente Wolf • Page 194: Tria Giovan • Page 195: Tria Giovan • Page 196: © Fernando Bengoechea/Beateworks/Corbis • Page 197: Peter Margonelli • Page 198 (left): William Waldron • Page 198 (right): Dominique Vorillon • Page 199: Thibault Jeanson • Page 200: William Waldron • Page 201: Dominique Vorillon • Page 202: Antoine Bootz • Page 203: © Fernando Bengoechea/Beateworks/Corbis • Page 204: Tim Street-Porter • Page 205: Pieter Estersohn • Page 206: Roger Davies • Page 207: Oberto Gili • Page 208: Luke White • Page 209: Colleen Duffley • Page 210: © Fernando Bengoechea/ Beateworks/Corbis • Page 211: © Fernando Bengoechea/Beateworks/Corbis • Page 212: Jonn Coolidge • Page 213: Mick Hales • Page 214: Thibault Jeanson • Page 215: Eric Piasecki • Page 216: Peter Margonelli • Page 217: © Fernando Bengoechea/Beateworks/Corbis • Page 218: Peter Murdock • Page 219: Tara Striano • Page 220: Jonn Coolidge • Page 221: Tim Beddow • Page 222: Richard Bryant/Arcaid – Designed by Calvin Tsao and Zack McKown • Page 223: Dana Gallagher • Page 224: Peter Margonelli • Page 225: Oberto Gili • Page 226: Tara Striano • Page 227: Tara Striano • Page 228: Tara Striano • Page 229: Tara Striano • Page 236: William Waldron • Page 239: Tara Striano • Page 241: Luke White • Page 242: Tim Street-Porter • Page 243: Antoine Bootz • Page 244: Brendan Paul • Page 245: Dominique Vorillon • Page 246: Jan Tham • Page 247: John M. Hall • Page 249: Laura Resen • Page 250: Peter Murdock • Page 251: William Waldron • Page 252: Oberto Gili • Page 253: Roger Davies • Page 254: John M. Hall • Page 255: Luke White • Page 256: John M. Hall • Page 257: Laura Resen • Page 258: Laura Resen • Page 259: © Fernando Bengoechea/Beateworks/Corbis • Page 260: Tara Striano • Page 261: Tara Striano

INDEX